BOB DYLAN

TOGETHER THROUGH LIFE

AMSCO PUBLICATIONS
a Part of The Music Sales Group
New York/London/Paris/Sydney/Copenhagen/Berlin/Tokyo/Madrid

Cover design: Coco Shinomiya
Photography: front cover-© Bruce Davidson/Magnum Photos
back cover-© Josef Koudelka/Magnum Photos
inside photos-Danny Clinch
Arrangements for publication by David Pearl
Project Editor: David Bradley

This book published 2009 by Amsco Publications,
A Division of Music Sales Corporation, New York

Order No. AM 997315
ISBN: 978-0-8256-3721-6

Exclusive Distributors:
Music Sales Corporation
257 Park Avenue South, New York, NY 10010 USA
Music Sales Limited
14-15 Berners Street, London W1T 3LJ England
Music Sales Pty. Limited
20 Resolution Drive, Caringbah, NSW 2229, Australia

Printed in the United States of America

BEYOND HERE LIES NOTHIN'

Music by Bob Dylan. Lyrics by Bob Dylan with Robert Hunter.

I love you pret - ty ba - by

You're the on - ly love I've ev - er known _

Just as long as you stay with me

The whole world _ is my throne _

Be - yond here _ lies

LIFE IS HARD

Music by Bob Dylan. Lyrics by Bob Dylan with Robert Hunter.

Slowly

The eve-ning winds are still   I've lost the way and will

Can't tell you where they went   I just know what they meant   I'm al-ways on my guard _

Ad-mit-ting life is hard _   With-out you near me

MY WIFE'S HOME TOWN

Music by Bob Dylan and Willie Dixon. Lyrics by Bob Dylan with Robert Hunter.

Well I didn't come here to deal with a dog-gone thing I just came here to hear the drummer's cymbal ring There ain't no way you can put me down I just want to say that Hell's my wife's home town

She can make you steal, __ make you rob __

Give you the hives, __ make you lose your job __ Make things bad, __ she can

make things worse __ She got stuff more po - tent than a gyp - sy curse __

One of these days, __ I'll end up on the run I'm pret - ty sure, __ she'll make me

IF YOU EVER GO TO HOUSTON

Music by Bob Dylan. Lyrics by Bob Dylan with Robert Hunter.

Additional lyrics

4. If you ever go to Dallas
   Say hello to Mary Anne
   Say I'm still pullin' on the trigger
   Hangin' on the best I can
   If you see her sister Lucy
   Say I'm sorry I'm not there
   Tell her other sister Betsy
   To pray the sinner's prayer

5. I got a restless fever
   Burnin' in my brain
   Got to keep ridin' forward
   Can't spoil the game
   The same way I leave here
   Will be the way that I came
   Got a restless fever
   Burnin' in my brain

6. Mr. Policeman
   Can you help me find my gal
   Last time I saw her
   Was at the Magnolia Hotel
   If you help me find her
   You can be my pal
   Mr. Policeman
   Can you help me find my gal

7. If you ever go to Austin
   Fort Worth or San Antone
   Find the bar rooms I got lost in
   And send my memories home
   Put my tears in a bottle
   Screw the top on tight
   If you ever go to Houston
   You better walk right

8. *Instrumental (fade)*

FORGETFUL HEART

Music by Bob Dylan. Lyrics by Bob Dylan with Robert Hunter.

Moderately

THIS DREAM OF YOU

Words and Music by Bob Dylan

JOLENE

Music by Bob Dylan. Lyrics by Bob Dylan with Robert Hunter.

I FEEL A CHANGE COMIN' ON

Music by Bob Dylan. Lyrics by Bob Dylan with Robert Hunter.

IT'S ALL GOOD

Music by Bob Dylan. Lyrics by Bob Dylan with Robert Hunter.

Don't make a bit of diff-'rence,   don't see why it should

But it's all right, __   'cause it's all good __

It's all good __   It's all __ good __

1.- 3.

3. Wives are leav-in' their

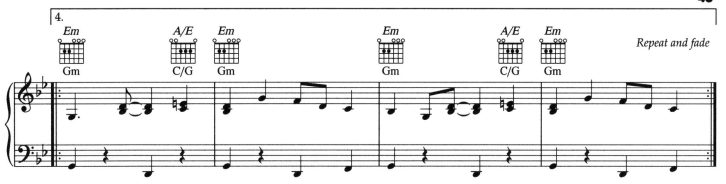

Repeat and fade

Additional lyrics

3. Wives are leavin' their husbands, they beginning to roam
   They leave the party and they never get home
   I wouldn't change it, even if I could
   You know what they say man, it's all good
   It's all good
   All good

4. Brick by brick, they tear you down
   A teacup of water is enough to drown
   You ought to know, if they could they would
   Whatever going down, it's all good
   All good
   Say it's all good

5. People in the country, people on the land
   Some of them so sick, they can hardly stand
   Everybody would move away, if they could
   It's hard to believe but it's all good
   Yeah

6. The widow's cry, the orphan's plea
   Everywhere you look, more misery
   Come along with me, babe, I wish you would
   You know what I'm sayin', it's all good
   All good
   I said it's all good
   All good

7. Cold-blooded killer, stalking the town
   Cop cars blinking, something bad going down
   Buildings are crumbling in the neighborhood
   But there's nothing to worry about, 'cause it's all good
   It's all good
   They say it's all good

8. I'll pluck off your beard and blow it in your face
   This time tomorrow I'll be rolling in your place
   I wouldn't change a thing even if I could
   You know what they say, they say it's all good
   It's all good

SHAKE SHAKE MAMA

Music by Bob Dylan. Lyrics by Bob Dylan with Robert Hunter.

Additional lyrics

4. Down by the river Judge Simpson walkin' around
   Down by the river Judge Simpson walkin' around
   Nothing shocks me more that that old clown

5. Some of you women you really know your stuff
   Some of you women you really know your stuff
   But your clothes are all torn and your language
      is a little too rough

6. Shake, shake mama, shake it 'til the break of day
   Shake, shake mama, shake it 'til the break of day
   I'm right here baby, I'm not that far away

7. I'm motherless, fatherless, almost friendless too
   I'm motherless, fatherless, almost friendless too
   It's Friday morning on Franklin Avenue

8. Shake, shake mama, raise your voice and pray
   Shake, shake mama, raise your voice and pray
   If you're goin' on home, better go the shortest way

9. *Instrumental (fade)*